E.C R.

Here and Hereafter

Thoughts and Suggestions

E.C R.

Here and Hereafter
Thoughts and Suggestions

ISBN/EAN: 9783743423206

Manufactured in Europe, USA, Canada, Australia, Japa

Cover: Foto ©Lupo / pixelio.de

Manufactured and distributed by brebook publishing software (www.brebook.com)

E.C R.

Here and Hereafter

HERE AND HEREAFTER

a

HERE AND HEREAFTER

THOUGHTS AND SUGGESTIONS

BY

E. C. R.

WITH A PREFACE BY THE

LORD BISHOP OF LINCOLN

RIVINGTONS
WATERLOO PLACE, LONDON
MDCCCLXXXVI

To the Memory of Her
Whose high spiritual Character and
Humble unselfish Life
Suggested many of the Thoughts contained
In this little Book.

"In the morning sow thy seed, and in the evening withhold not thine hand: for thou knowest not whether shall prosper, either this or that, or whether they both shall be alike good."

PREFACE.

It was one of the many wise sayings of Charles Marriott, whose "noble life" has been characterized as "a living commentary on the four Gospels," that "the right application of truisms is the better part of wisdom."

Hence many of us were grateful to Bishop Ellicott for offering us considerations, lines of thought, rather than arguments, in his lectures on the Being and Attributes of God.

Formulated arguments seem, at times, to limit the mind in its grasp of truth.

This is, I suppose, partly what is meant by the lines—

> "Ogni lingua per certo verria meno
> Per lo nostro sermone, e per la mente,
> Ch'hanno a tanto comprender poco seno."

The title of this little work is well chosen, "Thoughts and Suggestions," and the object of the writer would seem to be expressed in the words of the writer—to offer "thoughts and suggestions" which may "lead to fuller and deeper truth than they themselves present."

The thoughts are the thoughts of a reverent and healthy mind, possessing considerable insight into character, but singularly free from satire or bitterness of any kind. This is well shown in No. XLVII.:—

"Sharpness, satire, wit—these are telling and attractive gifts, and at times we thoroughly enjoy them. But in the long run, it is to the charitable that we turn."

The thoughts are chiefly confined to moral subjects, and hardly enter at all upon the domain of doctrine or religion; and yet they constantly lead upward in that direction, and this perhaps is just what moral reflections should do: according to the well-known conclusion—"So far therefore as a man is true to virtue, to veracity, and justice, to equity and charity, and the right of the case, in whatever he is concerned; so far he is on the side of the Divine administration and co-operates with it: and from hence, to such a man, arises naturally a secret satisfaction and sense of security, and implicit hope of somewhat further.

We are glad, therefore, to recommend this little work as thoughtful, pure, and true; and likely, we hope, by God's grace, to lead its thoughtful readers higher than itself.

E. LINCOLN.

January, 1886.

TO THE READER.

IT has been said that a good reader brings half the book himself, and in the case of the present one, the remark seems especially appropriate. For the writer only ventures to offer the thoughts contained in it, as suggestions;—mere outlines, to be corrected or filled up by the reader, and thus it is hoped to lead to fuller and deeper truth than they themselves present. This remark applies especially to those of a more imaginative or speculative kind. Those which are more practical in their aim make no claim to novelty or originality, and are only offered in the hope that as they have been written out of the fulness of the heart when most strongly felt, so they may appeal to the hearts of others and be of some slight use or comfort to them on particular occasions.

I.

Conflicting Duties (so-called).

WE are fond of talking of life with its conflicting duties, and pleasing ourselves with the notion that it is as complicated as the wards of an old-fashioned lock, full of turns and involutions. We are apt to forget that the best key is the simplest of all. It is called—a single mind.

II.

Humility.

It seems hard that the very grace said to be the most difficult to acquire should often make those who have won it of least account in the world.

If it be so in this life, humility will only cry the louder from the grave.

No force is ever lost. Sooner or later it will come upon us in all its power.

III.

Hero-Worship.

People are apt to be hard upon hero-worshippers. And certainly they do often expose themselves to ridicule from the jealousy, the selfishness, the fond idolatry with which the fervent admiration they feel, is mingled.

But take away the alloy, and what remains? A generous, a touching admiration for those whom they feel so far above themselves, of which their deriders are often incapable. Their hero-worship is a homage paid to goodness; their heroes, a personification of all that is noble. Disappointed they may indeed be here, but will not their happiness hereafter be in proportion to their capacity for reverence? What will be their rapture of joy when the Ideal of all that they admired here, is revealed to their sight!—when they behold the "Chiefest among ten thousand and altogether lovely," and to them the promise is fulfilled,

"Thine eyes shall see the King in His Beauty."

IV.

Love of Travel.

Some natures are filled with a craving for travel, which it seems hard should never be satisfied here. As they read descriptions of the wonders of art, the beauties of nature, the depth and glory of tropical skies, the brilliance of birds and flowers, the magic of old historic scenes,—their imagination is fired and they feel a restless longing to enjoy them. Others may do so, but to them the means are denied.

If this be the case with you, take comfort. Are you troubled because you cannot pass from one spot of this little sphere to another? What if hereafter your travels may be from star to star, from planet to planet! You may miss a few faint rays from the glorious sun of God's beauty, reflected here in some form of nature or of art. Hereafter you may behold the fair beauty of God Himself.

One journey at least awaits you—a journey the most inconceivable in its wonders,

Thou shalt, "behold the Land that is very far off."

V.

Capacity for Suffering.

If the pain of being grieved and wounded by our fellow-men, is in direct proportion to the love we bear them, what must be the pain caused by our sins to Him Whose love for us is greater than we can comprehend!

VI.

Humiliation.

Nothing is so humbling after a fall, as the remembrance of how well you looked in some one's eyes, before it.

VII.

Old Truths.

We think that we know perfectly certain commonplace truths, but our first personal realization of them comes to us with all the force of an original discovery.

VIII.

Helps by the Way.

God sends us many helps to raise us above the earthly desires, the mean and selfish thoughts, the low passions that weigh us down, into a higher and purer region. A beautiful picture, a moving strain of music, a fine poem, the sight of a face reflecting the goodness within, contact with a noble character, the story of an heroic deed, even our own self respect,—often act as ministering angels, true messengers of God to our souls. We think if only they could remain with us always, we could never act unworthily of their presence.

Passing helps they may be, but not all-sufficient. There are times in our lives, of sore trial and temptation, when there is only one support for our weakness, the knowledge that,

"The Eternal God is our refuge, and that underneath are the Everlasting Arms."

IX.

The Beauty of Holiness.

Because we are so dull that we must needs see with our bodily eyes that good is better than evil, God shows us on the faces of men how the one can beautify, how the other can disfigure.

X.

The Witness of the Face.

In certain sacred moments, we have seen on the faces of those whose lives have been moulded on the Life recorded in the Gospels, a look that we can only call unearthly, because we feel that it cannot belong to this world.

May we not take this look as a witness to the truth of Christianity? Could a delusion or a lie shed on any countenance such a light of peace and joy?

XI.

Thought.

Thought is wont to sleep in a calm, but the storms of life awaken it.

XII.

Facing Facts.

Look your troubles full in the face, and you will know what they are and how to meet them. Eye them with timid glance and shrinking step, like a horse shying at some object in the road, and you will always be afraid of them.

XIII.

Will Perfection be Monotony?

We sometimes say that we love our friends the more for their faults, because they are part of the character that is so dear to us. They would not be themselves, we say, without them. Then the thought comes over us, "Will not intercourse in the next life be dull and tame, when all faults have been toned away? Will not perfection itself be a wearisome monotony?"

But if faults are only the *mis*-direction of certain forces in the character, when those forces have been turned into their right channels, will not their strength remain? And if their strength remains, can the character be tame and insipid? And is not individuality an essence underlying all qualities and not dependent upon them,—one individuality differing from another, as much as do the diverse flavours of the various fruits of the earth? Some natures may have more of this distinctness of flavour, some less. But it will not be the attainment of their full perfection, which will make them dull and savourless.

XIV.

Test of Strength of Mind.

Few things are harder to bear than the vexations which might easily have been avoided. Just to miss some great pleasure when we might have had it for the lifting, so to speak, of our little finger ; just to meet with some annoyance when the slightest precaution would have stopped it, is a real aggravation of our disappointment.

Here comes in the test of strength of mind. The weak brood upon the annoyance till it becomes an exasperation that seems unendurable. The strong quickly close up every thoroughfare to the vexing subject, and drive their minds with firm hand and tight rein in quite another direction.

XV.

Human Judgment.

In judging others, we can all admire acts of charity to the poor ; laborious undertakings of which we can see the outward proofs. We hardly notice the apparently small sacrifices, the silence where a retort might have been made, the word of apology spoken, the little service done to one who has given provocation.

Trifles they may seem to us, and yet they may be as costly a sacrifice, as great a triumph of God's Grace. There may be compensating pleasures in the first case, nothing but pain in the second.

We smile at the simplicity of children who cannot understand the old puzzle of the pound of feathers being equal to the pound of lead; yet we cannot see ourselves that the many small duties and sacrifices of a quiet life may weigh as heavily in God's scales, as the heroic act of the great man who stands forth before the admiring gaze of the world.

XVI.

The Truer Kindness.

There is often far more love shown in letting another do a kind action, than in doing it ourselves.

XVII.

Over-criticism.

An over-critical spirit narrows the mind. The habit of looking out for what we can admire, both widens it and doubles our enjoyment.

XVIII.

Test of Charity.

It is generally a better test of true charity, a stronger proof of self-denial, to be kind to those a little below us in the social scale, or to those who are called "bores," dull, or uninteresting, than to the really poor.

XIX.

Under Trial.

We go to rest sometimes with an impression of guilt on our minds, because all day long we have been under trial, so that we feel as if evil had been with us continually. At other times night finds us calm and serene. All has gone smoothly, and we are pleased with ourselves and our neighbours.

And yet there may be a better record for the dark day than for the bright one, in God's Book of remembrance.

For temptation is not sin, nor its absence goodness.

XX.

Many Mansions.

It is easy to imagine some of our friends as having passed into the other life.

While they lived on earth, they seemed to care so little for its pleasures and interests, to live so much above it, that their removal into a world of spirits seems to us an easy transition.

But there are other people quite as good, as unselfish, as earnestly and sincerely religious, whom yet we cannot picture to ourselves in any other world than this;—the busy, bustling, practical folk, who take such innocent delight, in all the machinery of life.

Does not the existence of such characters suggest to our minds the suspicion, that some of our notions of the other state of being may be narrow or mistaken? Can we really believe that there will only be found scope for the Marys and none for the Marthas, in the blessed future?

XXI.

The Outer Court.

When thinking of the death-bed of some holy men and women, it is difficult to believe that the moment before they gently breathed their last, they were wholly in this world; the moment after, wholly in the other. Surely that look of unearthly peace on their faces, as they lay on their beds of suffering, shut out from the surrounding world, showed that their spirits were even then half in Heaven. Rather, might we say, that they had already entered into the outer court, before they were called into the nearer Presence of God.

XXII.

Royal Natures.

In every rank of life we meet occasionally the kings and queens of humanity. Perhaps their outward form, the cast of their features, corresponds with this nobility of nature. On no fairer work of God may the eye of man rest, where this correspondence exists. But even where it does not, we may trace in the expression of their faces, the presence of the royal nature. We feel that whatever faults might find entry into their hearts, the low rabble of vices would knock for entrance in vain. Such mean visitors as envy, craft, malice, spite, jealousy, would be spurned with contempt.

God allows us to meet sometimes with these noble natures, that admiring them, we may try to rise to their level.

But lest we should be too much discouraged by the contrast of our own pettiness and meanness, He has recorded for us the story of Jacob; to teach us how a nature, lowered by the meaner passions, may be raised and hallowed by His Grace.

XXIII.

Humour.

If it is impossible to believe that the charming gift which we call humour, comes to us from any low source, then it must come from a high one. If so, can we believe that there will be no scope for it in the next life?

Difficult as it may be to harmonize it with some of the notions current of a future life, is it not even more difficult to believe that we shall be deprived of such an innocent source of happiness?

XXIV.

Give to Babe.

We are sometimes afraid of giving our love to many, for fear we should thereby give less to each. Oh! vain and causeless fear! Does not love grow by exercise? And if He, in Whose image we were made, can love all without loss to any, the more we become conformed to His likeness, the more may we not hope to resemble Him in this?

There is only one kind of love that will diminish, and that is self-love.

XXV.

Pain.

There is good reason for our suffering more acutely through the pain we see others enduring than through our own; for we know the limits of the one by personal experience, while we know the other by imagination only, which has no fixed boundaries.

XXVI.

Becalmed.

You think that your spirit would always be unruffled, if you lived with certain kindly folk who never try you.

Yes.—But if in that still atmosphere your soul were becalmed, would you not pine for the rough breezes to blow her into port?

XXVII.

The Unexpected Message.

The deepest and most sacred thoughts of our departed friends often reach us in an unexpected manner. While they were with us, a delicate reserve hid from us the very essence, the great reality of their lives.

We take up a book that once belonged to them, and the mere stroke of a pencil, a date written against some favourite passage, reveals more to us of their inner life than we ever knew before.

XXVIII.

Gains and Losses of Sympathy.

Even from a selfish point of view, sympathy answers well. Without it we are reduced to the happiness of one. With it we have part of the enjoyment of every happy person we know.

But how about the sorrows? Will not sympathy force upon us also part of the sorrows of every sorrowful soul we meet? Yes, that is quite true; it cannot be denied.

But if it is also true that the greatest blessing may be found in sorrow, will not sympathy give us a share in that blessing?

XXIX.

Immortality of Goodness.

Oh marvellous! the undying power of goodness! I take up a book and read of some good action which so raises my spirit, that I feel braced to resist the first petty temptation that presents itself. But perhaps the man who performed it, lived hundreds or thousands of years ago. Perhaps he lived on the other side of the globe, and was separated from me not only by time and space, but by language, race, religion. And yet he has power now to change my purpose, to alter my life.

We think it wonderful that seeds, buried for thousands of years in the coffins of Egyptian mummies, should have power to germinate under the influences of earth and air; or that a ray of light, which left some far distant star thousands of years ago, should only now reach this earth. But what are these forces compared with the vital force of goodness?

XXX.

Human Opinion.

Some people seem only to live in the opinions of others. They feel clever or stupid, good or bad, according to their reading of the thoughts of those around them. Elated at one time, depressed at another, they have no independent basis of their own.

XXXI.

A Recipe.

Next time you feel irritated with any one, try and remember the time when you saw him at his best, and believe that the good which you recognized so clearly then, is still there, if only you could reach it.

XXXII.

Exceptions.

We are fond of saying that we can get over any faults in other people, except this, that, or the other.

If there were as many exceptions in our

Sovereign's Act of Indemnity, how many of our names would be found in it?

XXXIII.

A Hint.

It is almost a trite remark, how death glorifies the commonplace. We meet one day some person who seems dull, uninteresting, wearisome, and we congratulate ourselves if we escape from his company. The next day we hear that he has been suddenly called away from this known life, to enter into the mysterious unknown. How our thoughts about him are changed! The touch of death has transformed, not only his memory, but even his commonest possessions into something sacred. We think of his characteristics, of the latest sight we had of him, of our last exchange of words, with a new eagerness of interest. Do we congratulate ourselves now, on our escapes from his tediousness? No; we are trying to remember that once or twice we made an effort to listen to him with sympathy. Is there no hint for the future in this?

Perhaps this very day we might meet with some unfortunate, whom all avoid. So much the better for us if we do, for God would then be sending us an opportunity the sooner.

XXXIV.

Christ's Love.

What a blessing for us, that the special love of our Master for one of His disciples should have been recorded! It gives us ground for belief in the particular and individual nature of His love for each of us; it assures us that He does not love us in the mass, but separately.

XXXV.

The New Earth.

Perhaps we have been enjoying a pretty country scene in some quiet village, when golden rays of light are resting on the old Church tower, on waving corn fields, on the curly heads of merry children playing by the roadside. And then a feeling of sadness comes over us, as we think to ourselves that only in this earthly stage of our existence can we enjoy this familiar scene, so homelike, so natural. When our eyes close on this life, they can never look on the same again.

When thoughts like these pass over our minds like chilling clouds, then the promise of the new Earth, as well as of the new Heavens, comes to quicken our hope. Surely scenes like these cannot be amongst the "former things," which shall wholly and for ever pass away. If we believe that our resurrection body shall bear any relation to our present body—not identical, yet related—may we not also hope that the new Earth will bear the ennobled and glorified form of the old one? The same, yet better; all that marred it gone; all that beautified it, increased a hundredfold. The beauty we see now, but the little seedling from which the plant shall spring in perfect loveliness.

XXXVI.

Saints.

We have a feeling sometimes, when we are with those upon whom the light of God's Presence rests, that it would be well for us to enjoy all we can of their company here, since hereafter their place must be in a higher Heaven than we can hope to attain. But do we not hope to be in the Presence of the Holiest of all?

XXXVII.

A Blessing to Earn.

Do you ever remember the intensity of your feeling of love and gratitude, especially in childhood or youth, towards some one who spoke a kind word to you, or showed you sympathy, in some moment of shame and distress? Such a person won your heart for ever.

If to win gratitude be a blessing, how easily may that blessing be earned!

XXXVIII.

Half-heartedness.

If you wish all you do to seem dull and uninteresting, do it with half a heart and half your mind.

XXXIX.

The Personal Equation.

In making calculations from their observations of the heavens, astronomers are wont to make allowance for personal peculiarities of eyesight.

If people who know themselves to be thin-skinned would make a like personal equation whenever they feel hurt, half their affronts would vanish.

XL.

Good Manners.

You may erect a very elegant and showy edifice of good manners, but if you have not taken the trouble to dig the foundations deep in love and self-denial, your pretty little building will fall to pieces at the first strain of rough weather.

XLI.

Ill-temper.

Is there any personal discomfort so great as being in a bad temper? Put in the opposite scale the pain of the struggle against it, and see if that does not kick the beam.

XLII.

Vanity.

It is because the vain are morally so small of stature, that they brood so painfully over the wounds which they receive. Could they but grow a few inches, so as to be able to take a wider view of the world around them, they might forget their own sufferings in the discovery that all creation is not put out of gear, because their own obtrusive toes have been trodden upon.

XLIII.

Force of Character.

Such is the influence of strength of character, that it can make itself felt even in times of silence and inaction.

XLIV.

The Unfinished Picture.

We all of us carry about with us an unfinished picture, to which we add a few touches every day of our lives. It must be owned that it is less trouble to put them in badly than well. But it is worth while to remember, that as long as we live the picture must remain before our eyes. Some people manage to hold it in a flattering light, but they will be obliged to see it in a clear one some day.

XLV.

Society.

Those who allow themselves to be depressed by a sense of failure in society, are generally wanting in self-respect. They forget that whether they happened to be thought much of or little, they are just the same in themselves.

XLVI.

Dreams.

If we had not known it by experience, who would have imagined such a state of things as night brings to us. That the world should be withdrawn from us by a thick veil of darkness, and that we ourselves should either pass into what we might almost call a state of non-existence, since we are as unconscious as if we were inanimate; or else that we should find ourselves in scenes often so strange and unexpected, that they may bring us as great a change as if in our waking moments we had moved from place to place. If we except the occasional disturbance of bad dreams, what a really pleasant change from the worries of everyday life have not our dreams sometimes brought us!

XLVII.

"The Greatest of These."

Do we not continually prove by our own experience the truth of S. Paul's words, "the greatest of these is Charity"? Sharpness, satire, wit—these are telling and attractive gifts, and at times we thoroughly enjoy them. But in the long run, it is to the charitable that we turn. The assurance that they will take kindly views of us and of our neighbours is so comfortable. We feel that it is just their soothing presence that we need and must have. Is there any trait in the character of Solomon's virtuous woman more attractive than this,

"On her tongue is the law of kindness"?

XLVIII.

The Post of Honour.

"How hard the fight against the powers of darkness is to some, how seemingly easy to others!" we are tempted to cry. The enemy scarcely shows his front to them; and when he does, the attack is so weak that a very slight effort will turn him back, while we are in the hottest fight.

What! are we so chicken-hearted that we would ask for a safe and easy place, when to us has been granted the post of honour? Is not our spirit stirred, at the thought of grappling with the fiercest foes?—No; it is quite true that our Leader faced alone the whole army of darkness, but when it is our turn to fight for Him, we should be glad to be placed in some sheltered spot, where we should be quite secure from every attack and every danger.

XLIX.

Bracing.

There are some people who act upon our minds as a healthy refreshing sea-breeze on our bodies. The very sight of them, the sound of their voices, is invigorating. It would be well for us if we could be ordered into their presence when we need bracing, as we are ordered to the seaside for our health.

L.

Absent Friends.

When our thoughts are brimming over with love for absent friends, we have a feeling sometimes that they have such a force of their own that they must needs flow out and reach them. The hope springs up in our minds that they might carry them some blessing, bring them some comfort in trouble, or one of those sudden happy emotions that come to us all at times.

This may be but a fond fancy. But there is one way in which we may ensure that our thoughts should reach our friends in blessing. We may, by prayer, ask God to be our Messenger to speed them on their way to those we love.

LI.

Failure.

Even in the pain, which the sense of perpetual failure and imperfection gives us, there is comfort. It witnesses to us that at least we have some vision of what is better, some longing to attain to it. It speaks of a broken harmony and correspondence with all that is holy and perfect; and if the correspondence once existed, was it not a natural one; and if natural, might not He Who first established it renew it?

Apart from Revelation, the very pain speaks of hope.

LII.

Clear-sightedness of Children.

The clear-sightedness of children often surprises us. Setting aside half-explanations, refusing to gloss over difficulties, they aim straight at the heart of a question.

Does not this directness of vision spring from the perfect sincerity and truth of innocence? Where there is no guile to cloud the gaze, there truth can be seen as it really is.

Do we not see in children one illustration of the truth of the promise, " Blessed are the pure in heart, for they shall see God "?

LIII.

Human Nature.

Contrasts in human nature! Who would have believed them without experience? That the spirit of man should at one time rise, as on the wings of a dove, into the heaven of love and holy longings; and at another, grovel like a serpent in the dust of mean tempers and low desires.

Shall the serpent strangle the dove, as in the ancient emblems?—

With us lies the answer.

LIV.

A Homely Proverb.

"Nothing comes out of the sack but what was in it?" If we could but apply this homely proverb to the characters of our friends, instead of expecting from them what is not theirs to give, how much worry and disappointment we should be saved!

LV.

Stupidity.

Why not feel as much sympathy for the dull as for the sickly? Do not the feeble in mind often make as gallant an effort to carry on the business of life under adverse conditions, as the feeble in body?

Yet we pity the second and laugh at the first.

LVI.

Time.

Strange, that anything so accurately measured as the divisions of time, should be to us of such vague and variable dimensions, that a minute may be as an hour, an hour as a minute!

LVII.

Poets.

Poets crystallize the thoughts that other minds hold in solution.

LVIII.

Happiness.

Times of special happiness should be regarded as a sort of reserve fund, to be drawn upon in dark and cloudy days.

LIX.

The Tongue.

"There is that speaketh like the piercings of a sword."

Never is that sword so piercing as when taken up again by memory, and turned back into the heart of him who first used it.

LX.

Mental Gifts.

Some minds are like granaries full of rich stores, yet with no working power. Others are like the mills for grinding, strong in machinery, but containing no stores of their own. We look with admiration on the first, as endowed with special gifts from Heaven. The machinery of the second is dull to the eye, harsh to the ear, but it fits the treasures of the storehouse for the use of all.

Happy those who have storehouse and mill under the same roof!

LXI.

Music.

There are amongst the works of man some few which would almost seem to have escaped the taint of human imperfection; conceptions of poet, artist, architect, musician, in whose beauty the eye and the mind can discover no stain or flaw. If we may look for this perfection anywhere, most of all should we hope for it in music. For is it not in one sense the least material of all the arts? When we listen to some of the sublime strains of Handel, or of Beethoven, we ask ourselves, "Are they not perfect of their kind? Might we not listen to them in the courts of Heaven itself, and even there recognize their exquisite beauty?"

If this be so indeed, need we marvel at it? For if we are told that the Holy Spirit of God deigned to fill the minds of the workmen in his sanctuary in Mount Horeb to inspire them with designs for the hangings of the Tabernacle, is it presumptuous to believe that He might condescend to inspire the minds of those who were to leave us such glorious strains as Handel has left us in the Messiah,—strains that should comfort the mourners, strengthen the weak, and raise the souls of men from this sinful earth to the Heaven of hope and peace?

LXII.

Prayer.

Have you ever felt your life in sudden danger?

Let the fervour, the intensity of your cry to God for help then, be the standard by which to measure the earnestness of your prayers now.

LXIII.

Confidence.

Knock at another's heart, with sincerity in one hand, with kindness in the other, and confidence must soon open the door.

LXIV.

Slights.

When any one has shown us a discourtesy, our first feeling is that our own dignity has been wounded.

But it is the giver, not the receiver of a slight, who is lowered by it.

LXV.

Temptation.

Some people are so fenced in from certain temptations, that it is almost an impossibility that they should fall into them. Others are so besieged by them, that there would hardly seem a possibility of escape.—And yet there are found among the first class, those who dare to look down on the second.

LXVI.

The Truer Intimacy.

When we read the thoughts of some noble and gifted man who lived in former days, we think with eager longing, " What a privilege to have lived at the same time, in the same place with him ; to have seen him, to have known him ! "

And yet it is true that our acquaintance with him, may be more real, more deep, than that of those who were his daily companions. They may only have known him superficially ; while to us he has bequeathed his most sacred, his innermost thoughts, admitting us to an intimacy never dreamt of by them.

LXVII.

Magnanimity.

Who has not felt the restfulness of being with a magnanimous companion?—one who never takes offence, who thinks no evil, who is above all petty spite and envy?

It is the small passions that wear us out. We feel this when we meet with them in others. How much more when we meet them in our own hearts!

LXVIII.

Success a Certainty.

It ought to be a sufficient comfort to those people,—who, while longing to do some good in the world, honestly feel that they have no talents in the ordinary sense of the word, little personal weight or influence, and few opportunities,—to know that there is a way to the attainment of their desire, which offers no mere possibility or probability, but an unfailing certainty.

Nothing can conceal, nothing can utterly defeat, the influence upon others of that goodness which God's Grace can create in the character. The result of the effort to *do* good may be a total failure a hundred times. The result of the effort to *be* good, a total failure never!

LXIX.

Points of View.

It is easy to understand how different races of mankind should be unable to enter wholly into one another's thoughts and feelings. Their positions are so different that their point of view must vary. We expect too, to find this difference between nations of the same race. It does not at all surprise us, to find it even in families. But that no two members of the same family, no two children of the same parents, should be able to see any question in quite the same light, is harder to realize.

There is only One Who knows in very deed and truth, how each one of us thinks and feels. And our fears and our hopes rest on the faith that He does know.

LXX.

Unseen Presence.

There are times when the thought of the friends we have lost becomes so vivid, that we feel convinced that it is aroused, not by their image in the memory, but by their actual presence with us.

The truth of this belief can never be proved; but those who have felt it would say, that it is based on no creation of the fancy, but on an unanswerable conviction of the heart.

LXXI.

An Unforgiving Spirit.

How many Christians would be surprised to be told that they were unforgiving! But yet it is the truth. There is hardly anything about which we are so easily deceived. No doubt we would not injure those who have offended us; we might not only treat them with civility, but even bring ourselves to serve them;—and yet we have not really forgiven them. That we should think the same of their characters as we did before they committed the offence we resent, is often an impossibility. That we should make warm demonstrations of an affection that we do not feel, would be hypocrisy. But we allow ourselves with regard to them, an alienation of the spirit, an abandonment of fellowship, a shutting-up of the heart, that prove how far we are from forgiving them.

When we consider that so much stress is laid upon our forgiveness of others, that our pardon is declared to be dependent upon it, the question arises, Dare we, then, to call ourselves Christians? Might not a high-minded heathen bring himself to the point we have reached?—If we cannot go beyond it, let us beware how we profess Christianity; for certainly we do not make good our profession.

LXXII.

Our Own Character.

Do not spend labour in vain in trying to form yourself upon the model of every person you meet, who wins your admiration. Try and find out the plan which the Great Architect has traced of your character, and then build accordingly.

LXXIII.

Generosity.

If generosity sometimes seems to aggravate a wound, making us resent more keenly any unkindness shown to others, it will soon be the bringer of the balm to heal, for it will begin to whisper excuses even for the worst offender.

LXXIV.

Minds: Masculine and Feminine.

Women are not to blame, because they see faults as well as merits in the character of others, which are overlooked by men in the broader light in which they see them. Women's minds are like the plates of photographers which reproduce every detail. Or again, women are like long-sighted artists, who often see more than they wish of insignificant detail; while men have the advantage which artists with near-sight claim, of seeing what they look at, in its larger and more general effect. Men should remember this natural constitution of the feminine mind, before they condemn women as ungenerous; while women should be on their guard against dwelling so much upon details, as to be unable to see the whole.

LXXV.

The Angelic and the Saintly.

There seem to be two kinds of goodness, that we meet with in the world, to which we might give the names of the angelic and the saintly—the goodness of an essentially sweet and kindly nature, and the acquired goodness won through effort and struggle.

Though we may feel quite certain that none are so good by nature, but that they have some faults to subdue, yet most people would be able to say that they had, in the course of their lives, met with one or two persons, of a nature so unselfish, so lovable, so spiritual, that it would be difficult to think of any fault of which they could be accused.

Both kinds of goodness are attractive,—are beautiful; and when we meet with either, we may well thank God, that He allows us the help and the blessing of beholding it.

LXXVI.

Work.

Is not the keen delight which we take in doing any work, for which God has given us the special capacity—particularly in that kind of work which consists in creating or producing—a token to us that we are indeed formed in the Image of Him, Who looked upon His mighty work in the universe, and beheld that "it was very good;" and of Whom the Psalmist exclaims, after a magnificent description of the works of Nature, "The Lord shall rejoice in His Works."

LXXVII.

Kindnesses.

Some people are pleased with the kindnesses they receive, as proofs of the merits of the friends who show them;—others, as proofs of their own merits.

LXXVIII.

Two Worlds.

Tell us that all the outward world that we can see, and touch, and taste, is solid and substantial; and that the realm of faith, the spiritual world, is the region of dreams and shadows; and we can well believe it. But reverse this, and tell us that what seems so solid, is by comparison with the other, a mere outward show; and that the spiritual world, unknown to our senses, is the real and substantial one — and that seems a paradox indeed!

But does not the conviction of the truth of the paradox, grow more and more on our minds, as life advances and thought deepens?

LXXIX.

The Angelic Privilege.

We think that no created being was ever so blessed, as the Angel who was permitted to minister to the Saviour, in that most sacred hour of His Agony in the garden of Gethsemane; and the more our minds dwell upon it, the more unspeakable the privilege seems.

And yet, if we could but believe it, that privilege is ours. For, in order that not even the highest blessing which our hearts could desire, might be wanting to us, Our Lord has given us the assurance that whatever help or comfort we give to our brethren in their suffering, we do, indeed, give to Him.

LXXX.

Childhood in Heaven.

Is the idea of childhood, youth, and age, only an earthly one, springing from the present conditions of our corruptible bodies; or may we carry it beyond this world into that other state of being, when the immortal spirit shall inhabit the glorified body of the resurrection?

Such questions as these arise, when we think of those little ones, who have been summoned away from this life, in all the charm and innocence of childhood. Is it conceivable that we shall meet them hereafter, as we have known and loved them here; or shall we accept the idea of the poet, when speaking of the little one called away, he says—

> " Not as a child shall we again behold her,
> But when with rapture wild
> In our embraces we again enfold her,
> She will not be a child ;

> "But a fair maiden, in her Father's mansion,
> Clothed with celestial grace,
> And beautiful with all the soul's expansion
> Shall we behold her face?"

Revelation tells us nothing of this mystery; and thought, instead of groping her way into light by her searchings, only stumbles and loses herself in darker shadows. We cannot *know*; and yet when we try to picture any existence without children, we cannot but cling to the hope, that even in the world to come, there will be found souls peculiarly blessed, with a double portion of the gentleness, the candour, the trustfulness, the freshness, and the joyousness, which are the special graces of children here.

LXXXI.

Unequal Friendships.

In unequal friendships—unequal from inward, not from outward causes—it would seem at first sight as if the inferior were wholly the gainer: since he has so little to give in exchange for all he receives. But surely the admiration, the affection, the gratitude, the reverence, which he so eagerly offers in return, are of no mean weight in the balance.

LXXXII.

Facts.

We may load our minds with cart-loads of facts; but if the minds have not vital force enough, to extract the life-sustaining essence of wisdom from them, we shall be like some feeble-bodied warrior of the Middle Ages, groaning under the load of his heavy armour, and weakened and impeded thereby.

LXXXIII.

Jealousy.

If we might classify characters in their natural condition, unsanctified, unexpanded by the Love of God, we should say with regard to one fault—that of jealousy—that it is the second-rate characters that fall a prey to it. The third-rate are beneath it, because jealousy implies a power of loving, of which they are incapable. The first-rate are above it, because jealousy is a disease in love—love in its weakness and selfishness. The love of the highest natures is too deep, too strong, too pure, for such a feeling.

LXXXIV.

Is it too late?

When we reproach ourselves for unkind words and deeds towards those who have been taken from us, and long to atone for them, our first feeling is, that it is too late, that no efforts of ours can reach them now, and that it is not worth while to make them.

But do we know so certainly the condition of departed spirits, as to be able to assert, that it is impossible that they should know what passes amongst those whom they have loved? Even if this be the case, is there not the hope that in the meeting hereafter to which we look forward, all will be made known to them? And does not the thought of the possibility of thus adding to their bliss then, make every effort for their dear sakes, a comfort and a joy to our hearts now?

LXXXV.

Easy Generosity.

Generosity to our friends when they are in trouble, is a very cheap virtue. When our emotions of pity and tenderness are aroused, it is easy and pleasant to indulge them, even at the cost of a little self-sacrifice.

But how much sacrifice would we make for them, under ordinary circumstances?

LXXXVI.

Self-examination.

" The heart's aye, the part aye
That makes us right or wrang."

Would not Burn's couplet often be a better guide in the perplexities of self-examination, than pages of minute rules and tests, meant to supply us with moral scales, in which to weigh our conduct?

LXXXVII.

Self-deception.

Who would have believed that we could be so senseless, as first to offer our foes a becoming disguise and bestow on them high-sounding titles, and then, having thus thrown dust into our own eyes, invite them to take up their abode with us?

Yet how often when discontent comes to

visit us, we are pleased to call it depression; sloth, we name languor; touchiness, sensitiveness; ill-temper, indignation; and then, pleased with our own folly, open our fold to these wolves in sheep's clothing, and let them ravage there at their will.

LXXXVIII.

Growth of Thought.

Those who have watched the working of their own minds, must often have been puzzled by the irregularity with which thoughts come to them. There are times when the mind lies empty and barren: and there are times when thoughts crowd in upon it; and as we think of the strange irregularity, we wonder if there is any law which governs it.

Nature would seem to suggest an analogy. There is scarcely a spot of earth, in which you will not find the seeds of vegetation. Some will be full of them; others will have but few. There may be no sign of their existence on the surface, but when their season comes, they will burst into life. Even before that arrives, they may be forced into premature as well as into richer growth, by heavy showers of rain, by the stimulus of unwonted heat, by fertile soil brought to them from other ground.

Are not these things a parable? Do not thoughts—*when* first sown, we know not—lie buried and dormant in our minds, in greater or less abundance, awaiting the time when the course of our life's experience shall call them forth; or till the storms of sorrow, the stimulus of warm emotion, contact with kindred or with richer minds, shall quicken them and bid them spring up into flowers of beauty, and yield fruit to nourish and sustain, and to bear the seeds of future thought?

LXXXIX.

Judgments.

One would have thought that experience must have convinced us, if not of the sin, yet of the absurdity of judging others. The ignorance, the blunders, of other people with regard to ourselves, strike home with startling force to our minds. We know the shame which we have felt, when they have praised us for actions whose motives deserved blame; we know how their disapproval has disheartened us, when we were making the bravest struggle to do right. We feel how little they can know of our deepest feelings,—of our moments of fierce conflict, of passionate affection, of sharpest suffering.

There is nothing strange in this ignorance. But what *is* strange is, that in the very teeth of this experience, we should calmly sit in judgment on others, and self-complacently try to determine, the degree of their feelings, the depth or shallowness of their characters, the quality of their motives, and the precise measure of praise or blame which they deserve.

XC.

Capacity of Loving.

Those to whom has been given a large capacity of loving, have also received the responsibility of a revelation. Truths dim to them before, suddenly become clear. Through the deep feelings stirred by a true and warm friendship,—the hope, the joy, the admiration, the longing, the reverence for the human friend,—they may learn, if they will, what it must be to ascend into a still higher region, in which the soul hungers and thirsts after righteousness, is athirst for God, is in pain at the remembrance of grieving Him, rejoices to suffer for Him, delights to submit to Him, longs to be less unworthy of His friendship, pictures, though dimly, something of what the joy must be, of living in His Presence hereafter.

Those who have been thus taught, can enter into S. John's meaning when he asks, "He that loveth not his brother whom he hath seen, how can he love God, Whom he hath not seen?" Without the human, how can we enter into the Divine?

It may be indeed, that God pours the heavenly love more directly, and less through earthly channels, into some hearts than into others. But at least we may say, great is the happiness and great the responsibility, of those who have been thus taught.

XCI.

Pride.

It is when we feel most elated and triumphant through pride, that we may be at our lowest depth of abasement. Could we but see, with our bodily eyes, an image of our state, we might behold ourselves grovelling in the dust, under the over-mastering weight of a tyrannical monster, laughing to himself at the absurdity of our self-deception.

XCII.

Moods.

Without allowing ourselves to be the slaves of passing moods, it is impossible to escape from them altogether. We find our spirits buoyant with a feeling of happiness, or heavy with depression, warm or cold, energetic or inert, kindly or irritable, spiritual or worldly, according as the humour of the time takes us. We get to know our various moods so well, that we are inclined to take no pleasure in the happy feelings, because experience tells us they will soon pass away.

At least consolation for the dark thoughts, might also be drawn from that experience.

But cannot we use all our moods for our

own advantage, making virtues of necessity? Might we not draw from our happy moods, the spirit of gratitude; from our depression, humility and sympathy? Cannot we use our times of warm feeling, to spur us on to hearty service for others, and regard our times of coldness, as a sort of discipline to brace us, lest we should become enervated by emotion? Yes; even the attacks of sloth, of irritability, and of worldliness, might be used to win for us the resisting power of self-control.

XCIII:

Grumbling.

Better collect all your grievances and pour them out in one good grumble into the ear of a judicious friend,—if by that means you can clear your mind of them,—than suffer them to darken it, as dust and rubbish disfigure the pathway if left to lie upon it, instead of being swept into one big heap, and then carted away for ever.

XCIV.

Talents.

There are people in the world who fret their hearts away, because they feel they have powers for which they find no scope. Their natural talents they have tried to lay out to good interest, only to find no call for them, and disappointed and aggrieved they will labour no more.

Do they really believe that the Governor of the world will suffer a waste of power, which even we, in our earthly economy, should condemn? Even if here, they are to find no scope—and how can they be certain of that?—does not Eternity lie before them? If they have power to be rulers over five, or over ten, cities, are not the cities awaiting them? In that other Kingdom—together with the great company of those, who might never exercise all their talents here, since they were called away in the midst of their days—may they not hope for the great happiness of finding the work to do, for which the Giver of all good things has bestowed on them the capacity?

They shall find no waste there, of all the store that they have laid up here.

XCV.

Age and Youth.

Age need never fear that it will weary youth, if only it can retain its powers of love and of admiration. It may direct them into channels different from those of the young; but that need not debar true sympathy. If age cannot preserve an openness of the intellect to new thoughts and ideas, the openness of the heart is enough to maintain real companionship.

XCVI.

Our own Individuality.

We are so constituted that, however bad we may own the faults in our character to be, we cannot help feeling a sort of personal affection for ourselves. It is said that the plainest people would not wish to exchange faces, with those whom they most admire. They would like their own faces to be improved, but still they would wish to keep their own ; and it is the same thing with our characters.

Surely there is nothing wrong in this form of self-love! If our Creator thought our character worth designing, and saw that by His Grace something good might be made of it—and we could not doubt this, without doubting His love—why should we not feel a respect for our own individuality? It is this feeling that makes the theory of such complete absorption into another being, even the Highest, as would destroy this individuality, distressing to us. "Let me be joined to another better than myself, but let me still be myself," is the natural and surely innocent demand of our hearts.

XCVII.

The Divine Personality.

We have spoken of our own individuality; if it is this that we value in ourselves, it is this too that we prize in others. We may respect and admire their good qualities, but it is the self that underlies them, that we love. May we not even say that it is this that we love in the Highest of all. They felt it, who were with Him on earth, when they exclaimed, "Never man spake like this man." Does not the clear and original outline of His human character, traced for us in the Gospels, —His distinct, His unique Personality,—draw us with an attraction, independent of His perfect Wisdom, His perfect Holiness?

XCVIII.

Rejoicing.

Among our lost opportunities of happiness, we may well regret few more than our neglect of S. Paul's command, " Rejoice evermore," " Rejoice in the Lord alway, and again I say rejoice." Every now and then we have stepped out of the shades we have chosen, to realize, " What a joyful and pleasant thing it is to be thankful!"—when almost our whole lives might have been spent in the sunshine.

INDEX.

	NO.
Absent Friends	50
Age and Youth	95
Angelic and the Saintly, The	75
Angelic Privilege, The	79
Beauty of Holiness, The	9
Becalmed	26
Blessing to earn, A	37
Bracing	49
Capacity for Suffering	5
Capacity for Loving	90
Character, our own	72
Childhood in Heaven	80
Christ's Love	34
Clear-sightedness of Children	52
Confidence	63
Conflicting Duties (so-called)	1
Divine Personality, The	97
Dreams	46

	NO.
Easy Generosity	85
Exceptions	32
Facing Facts	12
Facts	82
Failure	51
Force of Character	43
Gains and Losses of Sympathy	28
Generosity	73
Give to Have	24
Good Manners	40
"Greatest of These, The"	47
Growth of Thought, The	88
Grumbling	93
Half-heartedness	38
Happiness	58
Helps by the Way	8
Hero-worship	3
Hint, A	33
Homely Proverb, A	54
Human Judgment	15
Human Nature	53
Human Opinion	30
Humiliation	2
Humility	6
Humour	23

	NO.
Ill-temper	41
Immortality of Goodness	28
"Is it too late?"	84
Jealousy	83
Judgments	89
Kindnesses	77
Love of Travel	4
Magnanimity	67
Many Mansions	20
Mental Gifts	60
Minds Masculine and Feminine	74
Moods	92
Music	61
New Earth, The	35
Old Truths	7
Our own Individuality	96
Outer Court, The	21
Over-Criticism	17
Pain	25
Personal Equation, The	39
Poets	57

	NO.
Points of View	69
Post of Honour	48
Prayer	62
Pride	91
Recipe	31
Rejoicing	98
Royal Natures	22
Saints	36
Self-Deception	87
Self-Examination	86
Slights	64
Society	45
Stupidity	55
Success a Certainty	68
Talents	94
Temptation	65
Test of Charity	18
Test of Strength of Mind	14
Thought	11
Time	56
Tongue, The	59
Truer Intimacy, The	66
Truer Kindness, The	16
Two Worlds	78
Under Trial	19

INDEX.

	NO
Unequal Friendships	81
Unexpected Message, The	27
Unfinished Picture, The	44
Unforgiving Spirit, An	71
Unseen Presence	70
Vanity	42
"Will Perfection be Monotony?"	13
Witness of the Face	10
Work	76

www.ingramcontent.com/pod-product-compliance
Lightning Source LLC
Chambersburg PA
CBHW020258090426
42735CB00009B/1136